THIS WRETCHED VESSEL

THIS WRETCHED VESSEL

Selections from
Lexington Poetry Month 2014

Edited By
Christopher McCurry
Hap Houlihan
and
Robin LaMer Rahija

Accents Publishing • Lexington, Kentucky • 2015

Copyright © 2014 by Accents Publishing
All rights reserved

Printed in the United States of America

Accents Publishing
Editors: Christopher McCurry, Hap Houlihan, Robin LaMer Rahija
Cover Image: *Nous Allons* by Theo Edmonds

Library of Congress Control Number: 2015940057
ISBN: 978-1-936628-35-3
First Edition

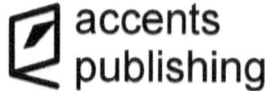

Accents Publishing is an independent press for brilliant voices. For a catalog of current and upcoming titles, please visit us on the Web at

www.accents-publishing.com

CONTENTS

Introduction / ix

Breath

BARE FEET / *Travis Stidham* / 3
CALLUSES / *Erin Mathews* / 4
CLOUDS BETWEEN US AND THE SPACE STATION / *Jim Lally* / 5
DROUGHT / *Allie Marini Batts* / 6
I'M LUCKY IT WAS RAINING / *Samantha Jean Moore* / 7
IN A FOREST / *Chuck Clenney* / 8
IN ANTICIPATION OF THE RIDING CROP / *tina andry* / 9
LIFELINE / *Jen Parks* / 10
LIKE MAGNETS / *Eric Scott Sutherland* / 11
MARRIAGE SONNET #3 / *Christopher McCurry* / 12
NO MATTER WHAT / *Jude Lally* / 13
ODE TO MY CEILING FAN / *Elizabeth Burton* / 14
OK CUPID THUNDER / *MC Spam Bot* / 16
A HOT CUP OF SUNDAY / *Michelle Knickerbocker* / 17
VIVA SAN FERMÍN! / *Leslie Bartley* / 18
PERFECT VIEW: DESCRIPTION OF A KING / *Shuntella Whitfield* / 19
PHASE ONE WOLF MOON / *Maggie Wells* / 20
PLUVIOPHILE / *Karah Stokes* / 21
RHAPSODY / *Sue Neufarth Howard* / 22
ROUTE 62, AGAIN / *Katie Riley* / 23
SHE AND THAT BLACK RESPLENDENT DOG / *Andres Ortiz* / 24
SILENT SPRING INTO SWING / *Jay St. Orts* / 29
THE COLORS OF SUMMER / *Alexis Tipton* / 30
THE QUIET RINGS / *Melva Sue Priddy* / 31
BLUEBERRY BLISS / *J W Mullins* / 32
TWENTY AND SINGLE / *Morghan Fuller* / 33
UPON APPROACHING 28 / *Taylor Emily Copeland* / 34
In the quarrels / *Jaria Gordon* / 35
AFTERMATH / *Julian DeVille* / 37
EXPLICATING THE EXPANSE OF SPIDER WEBS ... / *Sean L Corbin* / 38
FREQUENCY MODULATION / *Cheyenne Neckmonster* / 39
GASLIGHT / *J. Wise* / 40

AT SUMMER'S END / *Maggie Brewer* / 41
DRAFTING / *Jennifer Barricklow* / 42
DREAM CATCHER / *Jennifer Burchett* / 43
INTERROGATIONS (VI) / *Jenni B. Baker* / 44
ON WINGS OF LOVE PAGE 13 / *Robin LaMer Rahija* / 45
ROMULUS AND REMUS / *Andrew Depew* / 46
BAG LADY BALLET REDUX / *carole johnston* / 47
GENEROSITY / *Katerina Stoykova-Klemer* / 48
11:42 PM / *Matt Finley* / 49
VERDAUNTING / *hb elam* / 50

Eyes

A YOUNG GIRL'S GUIDE TO CRUELTY / *Victoria Sullivan* / 53
AN ANALYSIS OF STARGAZING / *Mattie Bruton* / 54
LISTENING TO SOUL / *Matt Spencer* / 56
BREAKFAST AT ZOTO'S / *Vijay Singh* / 58
DIALOGUE / *Bronson O'Quinn* / 59
DREAM FRAGMENTS / *Karen George* / 60
ENJAMBALAYA / *Deborah Adams Cooper* / 61
FREE WILL / *Amy Camuglia* / 62
GRANDE DAME / *Beatrice Underwood-Sweet* / 63
HOW TASTES CHANGE, OR DO THEY? / *Mary Allen* / 64
I MET GOD—SHE'S BLACK / *Bianca Spriggs* / 65
IN FAIR VERONA / *Jonel Sallee* / 66
LITTLE NO PEEP / *Catherine Perkins* / 67
LOATHSOME CREATURES / *Serena Devi* / 69
METAPOEM II / *Sayid Bnefsi* / 70
NAKED BODIES / *Rayny Palmer* / 71
ON AN OTHERWISE CLEAR CLOUD-LIT NIGHT / *Douglas Self* / 72
PALMOLIVE: ANNA AND JEAN-LUC / *Chloe Forsting* / 73
PASTORAL / *Gaby Bedetti* / 74
RED BIRD, BROWN BIRD / *Joan Burke* / 75
SHUT UP / *Marta Dorton* / 76
SOCCER IS LIFE / *Duke Gatsos* / 77
SOMETHING OF WILD HOLINESS III / *Kate Fadick* / 78
STORM INTERLUDE / *Roger Conner* / 79
SUNDAY PAPER / *K. Nicole Wilson* / 80
THE CAPTAIN DOES NOT UNDERSTAND … / *jeremy dae paden* / 81
THE CHILD OF A GOD NAMED GOD / *Tyler Worthington* / 82

THE PAINTED FOREST / Robert S. King / 85
THE SECTION / Erin Chandler / 87
THINKING OF LARGE NUMBERS / bront davis / 88
UNCLEAR COASTS / Joseph Allen Nichols / 89
i'm just sitting here. / meadow dawn smith / 90
WHAT LIES BENEATH / Pamela Gibbs Hirschler / 91
WHEN THE IDEA OF LOVE HOUNDS AROUND / Savannah Sipple / 92
WILD CANARY / Chaiya Miller / 93
YOU IN THE MORNING / Laurel Dixon / 94
MAN HOLDING BREATH IN OREGON … / Leigh Anne Hornfeldt / 95
KENTUCKY / S.R. Gollihue / 96
OFF THE TABLE / Linda Caldwell / 97
A QUESTION / Zlatna Kostova / 98

Memory

ANCESTRAL QUESTION / George Ella Lyon / 101
IN THEIR ELEMENT / Pat Owen / 102
USE FOR XANAX #212 / Keith Stewart / 103
WOMEN, BREAD AND BLOOD / Milena Valkanova / 104
It's midsummer's eve— / Barry George / 105
DOVES, GONE / Ann Neuser Lederer / 106
FAIRYTALE / Elizabeth Kilcoyne / 107
LETTING GO OF DICHOTOMIES … / Marvis Lisso Hartman / 108
FOOD DEPOSITORY OF CHICAGO / Rudy Thomas / 109
HARD / corey kirby / 110
ANTIPODE / Jay McCoy / 111
LIFE CYCLES AND HABITATS (A SEQUENCE) / Matthew Haughton / 112
FORGET-ME-NOTS / Nettie Farris / 114
PORTRAIT OF MY MOTHER AS A … / Pauletta Hansel / 116
FOUND IN HER BAGGAGE / Sherry Chandler / 117
FUNERAL WISHES OF A MODEST MAN / Ryan D. Mosley / 118
JOHN REID JUMPS AN IRON HORSE / David Cole / 119
LOST LOVE / Patrick Maloney / 120
ONE DAY I TOOK MY POEMS INTO … / Tina Parker / 121
POEM 10 / Elizabeth Beck / 122
REMEMBER WHEN / yahieisha adams / 123
REMEMBERED / Dennis Preston / 125
SEVEN MONTHS INTO FOREVER / Naomi Clewett / 126
SHE AIN'T EVEN FROM LEXINGTON / Liz Prather / 128

STROKE / *Nora Burton* / *129*
THE EDGE / *M J Eaton* / *130*
THE MOURNING WOMEN / *Kristy Horine* / *131*
THE WITCH'S HOUSE / *Kristine Nowak* / *133*
chipped fingernail polish / *Carmen Norris* / *134*
WRONG STATION, OLD NOTEBOOK / *Bernie Deville* / *135*
NOT AN EASY MAN TO LOVE / *Bobby Steve Baker* / *136*
ON TIME DILATION / *Eduardo Ballestero* / *137*

About the Poets / *139*

About the Editors / *149*

INTRODUCTION

If *Her Limestone Bones* can be read as a celebration of our first year writing as a community about the city and state that we love, then *This Wretched Vessel* shifts the lens to the people, past and present, here and gone, that have made Lexington and Kentucky the rich and vibrant place we know.

These poems, selected by Hap Houlihan, Robin LaMer Rahija, and myself are an exploration of corporeal existence, a look at the body, our ephemeral vessel. To be sure, there is much to praise about the body (agency and pleasure to name just two), but many of these poems strip it to its smallest parts—the breath, the eyes—then dissect it through memory. Here, after all, is the conflict: our bodies do not just carry us, they bind us.

And yet, almost to defy that fact, Lexington Poetry Month grows. One hundred and fifteen writers (up from seventy six in 2013) contributed to this year's anthology and produced nearly fifteen hundred poems; and so, whatever we are that isn't body, speaks through these poems as well. Whether it is love, history, belief, or memory these poems do not come to an agreement. Like with all good collections, *This Wretched Vessel* asks us, individually, to seek what is beyond the body by poking and prodding the tenderness of this life that each poem presents.

It helps to know that others are seeking with us, that not only did poets and editors come together to make this collection possible, but community leaders and business owners who support the organization and production of this project. Because of them, and because of you, Lexington Poetry Month lives on in 2015.

—Christopher McCurry

For a complete list of participating poets and their submissions, visit accents-publishing.com/blog/lpm-2014-registrants/

Breath

BARE FEET
Travis Stidham

today I saw just a little
girl dancing on the hood
of her mother's car so

today I thought Whitesnake
I thought about all
the videos of women shaking
everything about themselves

and I thought about all
the girls growing up too quickly
in back seats and under school
bleachers

I can't remember the last
time I was a woman
but remembered crawling over
an old green car to peep
over the cab at the soldiers
on the other side

today I saw a little girl
dirty bare feet naked to the world
on a rusted car in the lot

for all I know
this is the only stage
the only dance practice
she'll know

CALLUSES
Erin Mathews

black grit
crusts my feet.
hardened from miles
of walking barefoot,
brother and dogs in tow.

weaving through yards
over curbs, we form
a mass of roving limbs and leashes.
disentangling in a familiar dance

under street lights
we pull apart
all the things that
eat away at us in daylight

leashes burning our wrists,
night air sticky at our backs,
we roam.

CLOUDS BETWEEN US AND THE SPACE STATION
Jim Lally

She sleeps on the couch in a red dress
pulled up to catch the night air
a small alarm sounds out the approach
of the space station
its longest showing
since Christmas
and I hover over her murmurings
like a NASA priest hoping for another launch

The play of my hands
the points of my reference enfolded
in her dreams
weightless
and blue like the oceans
not enough to disturb her orbit
so alone I exit to the sky's gray dress
pulled down to avoid the eyes of fireflies

DROUGHT
Allie Marini Batts

Every day ripe corn lingers
in the field unpicked:
silk, more brittle in the sun
husk, papery from the heat
cob, like bone—no rain on the horizon—
rows of kernels puckering,
until the corn prays
for even earworms and flea beetles to come,
lest it fall back to the dirt
untasted

I'M LUCKY IT WAS RAINING
Samantha Jean Moore

'cuz I 'bout caught flame
when you came
looking through my window

IN A FOREST
Chuck Clenney

Making out
In the forest
Is great.

Evident ecological decay;
Turning into life
And love.

Beautiful bird songs,
Scents of sap,
Ideal isolation.

Who cares if
Your butt
Gets dirty?

IN ANTICIPATION OF THE RIDING CROP
tina andry

haunches quivering
like a race horse
who knows
he has
to submit
and be whipped
if he ever wants
to win.

LIFELINE
Jen Parks

If you look close,
you can still see the line—
it's still there.

You can trace it,
faded and brown—
the color of dry earth
before a summer rain.

A timeline
with only one event.
Before and after.

A demarcation between
innocence and discovery;
between barren hope
and the joyous cries
of life.

One by one,
I placed your wet,
new body against mine,
your lips finding my breast,
the cord pulse slowing.

And I wept—
at our inevitable
separation.

LIKE MAGNETS
Eric Scott Sutherland

Like Magnets
we are drawn
to the depths
of each other
unable to stave
off the impending
collision. The heat
immense in the small
space that separates
the fleshy vessels
we find ourselves
in, too weak
to fight the pull.

MARRIAGE SONNET # 3
Christopher McCurry

You've been
letting
your hair
grow

and
goddam
if it doesn't
make a

shirt
tearing
chest
beating

savage
out of me.

NO MATTER WHAT
Jude Lally

I do
I just
Can't escape
This broken body

This wretched vessel
This doomed life boat
That nobody wants
And nobody should be

Assigned to, subjected to
Especially women and children
Whose fate would be demise
To wind up swimming with cinder blocks

Sunk, stuck
On the bottom of the sea floor
Looking up at life
Watching the gulls drift by

In the open blue
They'd be envious
Of the living, of the breathing
And, at night

Of the twinkling stars
Burning zillions of miles away
Their presence hidden
Only by daylight

And no signal strong enough
To hear the call for help
For once a body is capsized
The mind is sure to follow

ODE TO MY CEILING FAN
Elizabeth Burton

> There is something dangerous about the boredom of teenage girls.
>
> —Megan Abbott

The days always get hotter
When you have less
To do with them. The heat
Buzzes and hems you in,
Makes your skin sticky
And peppery, like some kind
Of exotic fruit, ready
To be picked.

Empty hours stretch
In front of me like a desert,
Stretching lazily, cat-like,
And I let the peculiarly sultry
Air of Kentucky in the summer
Wrap me up like a cocoon.
I'll only be a teenage girl
For another year, and I wonder
If, when I pull into that third
Decade like a crooked
Parking space, I'll no longer
Spend hours staring at the ceiling,
Feeling inexplicably
Like I should be smoking
A cigarette.

The gravity of the things
I could be doing pulls down
My limbs and makes me feel drunk,
Like I'm heavy enough to pin

Someone down and keep them
Underneath me forever.

This must be why everyone
Is so eager to write teenage
Girls off, this carefully concealed
Potential, coiled in my muscles
Like snakes. If I could somehow
Keep the magnolias from opening
And saturating the air,
If I could keep the bees from buzzing,
Then I would be a terror to see.

OK CUPID THUNDER
MC Spam Bot

You can definitely see
the expertise
within the paintings
you write.

The sector hopes
for even more
passionate writers
like you
who are not afraid to say how they believe.

At all times follow your heart.

Golf and sex are the only things …

A HOT CUP OF SUNDAY
Michelle Knickerbocker

Juicy orange aroma bright
flicker mouth waters book face
surprise movement gentle cat nudge
jumps down touching elbow desk flat
character top Magic tape straps
pieces to pieces of paper art
into envelopes waiting
to drift slowly hand to hand
delivered to transfer ground pride
strong brewed hot drink sweet spicy rent
meat of my life pays the bills.

VIVA SAN FERMÍN!
Leslie Bartley

I wanted to write a nice poem for Monday
but only 4000 miles away my girlfriend is losing her mother.
She's spitting Spanish insults, saliva-first at her only child
for kissing me just 4000 miles ago

A fighting bull reference would be too obvious here
but I've never met this woman and could charge at her, snorting up dirt
    for 903 whole yards
right into the bullring
and I can't believe this shit still happens

I'm only granted tonguey screeches from this woman across the ocean,
laptop first, 6 hours difference
and make myself feel better by imagining her as a giant fire-eyed squid
surfacing from the Atlantic between us, lashing at waves instead
of my girlfriend

Because I barely remember 13-year-old me
croaking "I'm gay" to my mother but will never not write about
what came after

the pathetic symmetry
of trying to climb into our mother's beds nine years apart
and with a cracking disregard, were turned away because of a breathy
    spring kiss

PERFECT VIEW: DESCRIPTION OF A KING
Shuntella Whitfield

Black T-shirt.
Grey warm-up pants.
Grey Nikes—size 14.
Lips so succulent you want to bite them.
Seductive brown eyes.
Broad quarterback shoulders.
Hand-carved chiseled chest.
Beautifully cut massive arms.
Tight round ass.

God was clearly just showing off when he made this King.

PHASE ONE WOLF MOON
Maggie Wells

From my window I can see his eyes,
lantern-bright,
in the wine-deep darkness of the trees at sunset.
As we stare I wonder if the
stutter
hitch of my heart is
fear
or anticipation.

PLUVIOPHILE
Karah Stokes

The rain loves me. It fills my every cell,
plumps me until I'm smooth and ripe.
It lifts me in its floodwaters.
It washes me clean, dilutes
the poisons in my veins.

My capillaries are the rain's tiny highways,
rivers that nourish and drain
miniature fields and farms,
forests and mountains.

When I am farthest away from them,
the rivers flash like forked lightning,
remind me I am water's offspring,
the rain's own child. That I belong to them.

RHAPSODY
Sue Neufarth Howard

Barefoot in the
moonly garden
electric blue
luminous dusk
fireflies sparking
whirring wind has
willows dancing
by the ripply
rushing river
lacy clouds are
garlanding the
emerging stars
birds' fiesta
winding down slow
secrets, poem fresh
spill into the
silvering air
caught in a web
of wistful thought
I will ripen
through night dreams to
ballad of love.

ROUTE 62, AGAIN
Katie Riley

On my motorcycle, I fly along twin parallel lines
and pass a box turtle stalled out
in the middle of the road.

I slow down and turn back
and then shut down the bike and leave it.

My bulbous head is heavy and my breath
sticks to the face shield. Sweat runs over
my skin and under the skid plates

of the jacket. Even my jeans sour to the crevices
of my knees as my heavy boots clunk against
the road.

I pick up the turtle as he battens down
his casings. His underside is white, combed
with black veins and scuffed where he'd been knocked
across the asphalt.

Two drops of blood leak from him: brighter red
and thinner than my own

that pooled yesterday from my finger
and I licked away.

I carried him the direction he was heading,
and placed him under cover of tall clover—
and

hoped death would become confused
by the sudden disappearance of his trail
and would follow the yellow lines instead.

SHE AND THAT BLACK RESPLENDENT DOG
Andres Ortiz

She and that black resplendent dog.
She had read some Hermann Hesse shit, and had an artisanal handbag,
a nice face, and a big and good-looking ass,
a ring in her nose, and clean hands,
"maybe she washes her hands, twenty times a day" I thought,
her hands were clean, more clean that anything I had seen before,
clean, as ivory, or something like that,
in these times I was (or I pretended to be) some kind of classical musician,
for that reason (obviously) I was inconsolably unhappy,
but her hands,
"she could transform lead into alchemic gold," I thought,
"maybe for that reason her hands are so clean."
Then a miracle occurred,
there was a fierce battle in the heavens, and some celestial warrior (an angel, demon or ibis),
fell down under the door of the train station,
and she couldn't go inside the wagon,
neither could I,
so I talked to her,
and she talked with me,
and in some place in the ocean, a boat beat the storm and found the land.
I met her again, a couple times after this night,
for causality, it was a design or some shit like that.
She was an architecture student in some exclusive private university,
she had these cute expensive clothes,
and all these awesome perfect friends with perfect lives, nice cars,
and parents paying their motherfucking bills,
I couldn't afford even public school, in fact I gave guitar lessons to live,
and I pretended to be a musician,

(In that time I had some kind of loser ambition about writing a fantastic symphony,
telling the history of the secret reasons for Pilato to ask Jesus "what is the truth?")
and of course, I had all this Oliver Twist shit over me,
but she, she lived in a bubble, (she told me after that her father had been a motherfucker abuser).
Some people don't understand how things work in South America,
there are all these invisible walls, dividing the people,
It's a little picturesque hell, with tourists taking pictures of all the miserables,
serving the riche bastards.
That was my city.
And that was my little labyrinth in that moment
(I would know others after that).
She talked with me about her paints, her pictures,
the homeless dogs that she'd feed at night,
her simple deductions about her university classes,
her favorite French theorizers,
that talked about the injustice of the war in Algeria,
that denounced the evil Vietnam War,
and she, of course she was indignant
for all these awful things that were 50 years ago,
oh, she was an idealist, a beautiful idealistic girl,
with perfectly clean hands,
with three maids in her home,
with a beloved imported cat from Norway,
And I told her,
About the finite permutations of the natural harmonics,
About a black horse that comes to me in dreams, and his fantastic eyes of fire,
About my obsession with the last hours of Judas,

and his personal crusade allowing the Messiah's execution, to save the cosmos,
About the salt in the fields of Cartago,
About Thomas Aquinus and Dante Alighieri, creating cathedrals of words,
superior and more durable than rock,
About inconmensurables waterpipe cities in the land of Arminia,
About the wall that stopped Alexander the Great beyond India,
About my personal suspicion that we all are a dream inside another dream,
About a foreigner that killed some Arab guy "because of the sun,"
I talked too much, because I had a lot to say, and she listened to me,
And one night, the inevitable happened.
She and I were walking in the clear night of Quito,
And the sidewalks became chess tables,
I swear it,
And I understood that Kierkegaard said, about the infinitude of the instant
(Maybe I am still there, pretending to be a tower).
Then, we both sat outside his home.
And from the darkness a huge black dog came to us,
Was a bright animal, enormous, magic, shining in his blackness,
Was the dog that came night after night, to her door,
To kiss her perfect hands, and receive food and water,
was her adopted homeless son,
the mystic animal came and lay in front us.
Of course I put my hands over it.
And she did the same.
In some moment, we touched hands,
we touched hands,
since that night we continued touching each other,
in those days , I loved the fucking rain,

what fantastic and cold drops of water come from the sky, I thought.
I wrote dark and fantastic histories about angels that had philosophical reflections about their own faith and the itineraries of all the birds in the world,
I wrote histories about ancient languages created through the angles of the Indian pyramids,
I wrote histories about lovers who traveled to Greece to find the truth, in a circular sesame bread,
But, with the days, the months and the moons the fur of the black dog was shedding.
The animal got sick,
and at the same time, she and her perfect hands were starting to get far from me,
That was like a change of season, slow but inevitable,
she had this perfect world, of exclusive universities,
good looking friends with expensive clothes, and nice cars,
and of course,
finally the dog died.
And, we (or part of us) died with this marvelous animal.
I never saw her again,
After that, I continued having amazing dreams
About mystic horses that visited me in vivid dreams, with eyes of fire.
And my heart continued being tormented with the doubt of Pilato, about the truth,
and the silence of Christ after the question.
I quit the music, and I got a costume
to sneak myself into some kind of academic circus,
like a fake oracle about the present,
I drank with the outsiders, whores, harlots,
and taxi drivers who dance like drag queens at night,
I have hired prostitutes to have somebody to talk with,
I have sold my ideas and thinking to the wrong persons, to pay the bills,

I pretended to be in love, and some women pretended to be in love with me,
But,
Sometimes, when I can't sleep,
I remember that enormous dog,
walking beside me and protecting me from the night,
all the road from her house to my city room,
I remember this wonderful animal
Its resplendent black fur,
And she, and her perfect hands
On it ….

SILENT SPRING INTO SWING

Jay St. Orts

> The birds are singing. The bees are trying to have sex with them, as is my understanding.
>
> —B. Simpson

The possums do it angry-style in the backyard; The worms are gooily clinched up around front.

Christ, folks, I am trying to mow the grass for crying-out-loud. Speaking of …

Cats shrilly scream at each other while in the throes of kitty passion—waking me up (again); At *least* two dogs are up to something in the alley, and I don't think it's playing with a bone (ahem).

But at least one bedroom, makeshift or otherwise, remains utterly silent.

THE COLORS OF SUMMER
Alexis Tipton

Looking down the street
I see the vibrant yellows
And the vivid reds.
The colors of the tulips everyone seems to have planted.
The grass, a bright green.
It wears the badge of health.
The countless shades of green that make up the leaves on the trees
Dance in the slow summer breeze.
I take a deep breath
And let out a deep sigh.
Summer is finally here.

THE QUIET RINGS
Melva Sue Priddy

longing for zinnias and marigolds
to burst reds and oranges,
the sunflowers to smile
yellows reds and chocolate
nodding yes yes
and yes. All their green
arms waving to satisfy
what the wind requires.
For now leaves'
bitten edges
sitting with feet, theirs
and mine, in savory soil.

BLUEBERRY BLISS
J W Mullins

With anticipation they linger
Tender and ripe
Bursting with giggles and sighs
Supple and sweet
Eager fingers are stained
With the joy that remains

TWENTY AND SINGLE
Morghan Fuller

When every other hand is being held, it's easy to find yourself reaching into the void.
Settling seems simpler than waiting for what may never come,
And if you wake up in a stranger's bed enough, surely you can make it feel like home.
If someone calls you baby a few days in a row, the word can mute out insincerity.
You can ignore the venom someone spits if they can make their kisses sweet enough.
If you pick your clothes up off enough bedroom floors, you can convince yourself that this is a staple of growing up.
You can lift bottles to your lips, and inhale smoke into your lungs, and say that you're living the life.
But when everyone is coupled up, it's easy to feel like you're the sock in the drawer without a match,
And it's easier to find frat parties than it is to tell someone you're scared shitless that you'll die alone.

UPON APPROACHING 28
Taylor Emily Copeland

I shed people like work clothes—
each one falling to the carpet,
immobile, silent—find peace
behind a wall of words.
I am not creased yet. My eyes
still brown bulleted focus.
I could look twenty-three for
a while longer. I could count
the remaining beats of my heart.

* * *

Jaria Gordon

In the quarrels
of a triple-stalled Salvation
Army shit room a 16-year-old white girl
crushes her mommas rocks
for her on the rim
of a handicap toilet.

I trample into her first
rigid near gagging
my suspicion as she hurriedly
dusts the undersides of her palms
on crockery thighs not nearly as pristine
as the residues left there.

Hungrily we mourn
no losses of perceived youth for shame
loosely we scamper cringing into silent
departures worn well between strangers
picking the other apart
neither nearly as far away from yesterday
as home

she begs me not to snitch
with a shifty hi sidestep
I beg her not to ask me why I do
because a mother should be moon
not a waving desperate desolation
on the eve of any youth.

Her mommas tired breast nipples poke out at me
in a clinging pink shirt around the wall edge I
watch them a cougar reminiscing of tender joys
or dormancies but more likely of the refusals

we bear in lieu of optimistic delusions
white girl and I are waiting for something more
her of her mother I of the world in me
we are each neither naïve

nor burst
our wombs bleed but with only small knowings
her momma screeching and handcuffed
do not startle a caged raven and an onyx barn owl
cleaving soft whispers
weeping curses across a tundra
of differences for example her eyes prick
back down a hallway at me in a place where shelter
is only a pagan idol in name
and I am not afraid
of her neither she of leaving
there is no place unlike starving
or asphyxiating inside
your own family
or on earth

AFTERMATH
Julian DeVille

you know the
        sky is a nitrogen haze
reflected in your partly-cloudy eyes
gasses floating in space
a mirror coat deflecting
atomic barrages from an
illimitable number of footsteps away,
and I know somewhere
        in the heterogeneous aftermath
organic juggernauts grazing
and machines in the garden whirring
to brew chromosomes and nectar
rests my personal forecast,
reflected in your phosphate pupils

EXPLICATING THE EXPANSE OF SPIDER WEBS ON THE PORCH OF OUR APARTMENT
Sean L Corbin

Spun across the twilight and porch light
and erudite examples of semi-quality carpentry

and littered with lines from a linguistics
illuminated only by an instinct and more legs
than you could shake a katydid at

and congressing with community centers
of a census of separate yet equal species

and catching our child's eye just past dawn
by turning drips of sun into kaleidoscopic cartoons
concerning the capture of criminal caterpillars

and drooping in the evening wind and wild
tobacco smoke only to be wound again
by another deposition of dew

and regenerating with each enriched consumption
and conversation with the crowns of our heads,

these webs are the rings on our fingers.

FREQUENCY MODULATION
Cheyenne Neckmonster

playing records,
speaking alone
in a half-dark room,
listening to myself talk

that incessant mechanical chirp.

knowing others are listening
hell, maybe thousands of them,
but most of us will never meet.

i've been doing this
once a week
for years.

in everyday conversation
or when my name is given for a table,
sometimes people say

'oh! are you cheyenne from the radio?'

and i am baffled,
delighted, ignited, excited
and grateful that life has
led me to this place,
this decade,
this universe
to share reproductions
of people doing things alone
in half-dark rooms,
listening to themselves.

GASLIGHT
J. Wise

My love is a violence
to which he has not consented.
You can't say these things to me, he says.
I tell him I won't call him for a while
so I can calm down, that I needed him
not to call me,
not to ask anything of me,
because whatever it was we did those other weekends
wasn't nothing, no matter how many times
he repeated it.
Two weeks later
he texts just to ask
if you can buy beer on Sunday in Danville.
I say no.
An hour later he calls
to laugh and let me know that I had been wrong.
I laugh back, and talk and sigh,
mad that he broke my silence, but
relieved to hear his voice.
I'm sure he'd still deny
it flickers nervous
like a gaslight
as he speaks to me—
but then, who am I to talk?
I'm already back to pretending
that my voice is steady, too.

AT SUMMER'S END
Maggie Brewer

I check the "single" box and
slide my wedding ring
over to my
right hand.

Today
you are my wife,
but tomorrow
you will be
my roommate
again.

It doesn't matter
what the law says,
the reverend blessed,
our hearts know
if the wrong parent
gets wind
of who
their child's
teacher
loves.

DRAFTING
Jennifer Barricklow

today a sinuous slipstream of poems
roared onto the straightaway
each drawing the one that followed
so close there was no wake
each pushing the one before
ever faster toward the finish

DREAM CATCHER
Jennifer Burchett

She sleeps with one foot outside the covers, always has.
> Brave scout in the night
> testing the air;
> the King's taster.

An unlikely talisman, with its calloused heel and chipped coat of
> fire engine red.
> Hardly a formidable front line
> but still.

A toe ripples the surface of the still-dripping watercolor of night dreams
> born of daydreams
> born of fear and grief
> and hope.

INTERROGATIONS (VI)
Jenni B. Baker

Do you make relationships difficult? Do you sense a resistance? Do you feel more or less isolated now? Do you ever feel lonely? Do you consider yourself vulnerable? Do you feel 'visceral' is an accurate description? Do you have a stance in confronting somebody else? Do you still believe that? Do you?

ON WINGS OF LOVE PAGE 13
Robin LaMer Rahija

Bob unlocked
         Katie, and she
smiled
     Katie couldn't help thinking how
        the ads promised
           a move up the hierarchy.

ROMULUS AND REMUS
Andrew Depew

After the farmer killed the wolf
he ripped the babes from her breast
and turned her into a warm blanket
so that she would always be close.

If they'd stayed with the wolf
would we be flossing blood from our teeth
instead of washing from our hands
the gore that all great empires are built from.

BAG LADY BALLET REDUX
carole johnston

once I was
(will be) a bag lady
busking poems
on the street for coffee
one haiku for a cup

always knew
someday I'd lose it
(losing it)
bags of amygdala
in a shopping cart

GENEROSITY
Katerina Stoykova-Klemer

Kentucky asks me
to marry him. I do.

Kentucky allows me
to keep calling Bulgaria

my country.
Bulgaria seems happy

with whatever I give her.
I seem happy

to miss her.

11:42 PM
Matt Finley

We meet again.
That special time
when I'm short on sleep
and long on task.
I'm rushing to bed,
to lie and sweat.
A to-do grows longer
and longer,
but you're always short,
anxious, and moving on,
like me
after an hour or two
of fretting over this
and that
and a poem I should write.
Wait for me.
It's no use.
11:46 pm is here,
and she's meaner than you.
I wish I knew what I had
before it ticked away.

VERDAUNTING
hb elam

the green screams through the hospital window
a shrill, heard through my eyes
quite silently
quite silently
the word comes to me
verdaunting
the panic of life
yet lived, in bloom,
the hair of the trees yet to fall off,
instead, sprouting out and up
seeking sun
seeking some sun
seeking some life
that has not yet become theirs

Trees, in threes, beat a drum
to a rhythm intangible—
a soldier's call, a baby's cry,
covered and jaded deaths
of any & all things

walking to the car I feel the trees
watching
as I get in and drive
away
a way
from them, into them
into a summer of
possibilities

tamed by their verdant dreams of spring

Eyes

A YOUNG GIRL'S GUIDE TO CRUELTY
Victoria Sullivan

age six—two girls
pin me back against
a chain-link fence

age eight—girl
takes safety scissors
to our paper-thin friendship

age ten—girl calls
english teacher fat
she quits by year's end

age twelve—girl rips
shirt from the bruised
breasts of another

age thirteen—girls
use words i don't understand
i laugh anyway

age sixteen—girls
whisper, i grind my teeth
until i am deaf

age twenty-one—girl
walks past and i
think i might hate her

AN ANALYSIS OF STARGAZING
Mattie Bruton

Aquarius, the water bearer,
cradles my French horn Grecianly
and pours a fountain of youthful spit
onto the floor of the seventh-grade band room.
(The carpet is pomegranate red tonight,
                             symbolizing temptation.
   The spit is cold tonight,
                             symbolizing regretted reasons
                             I did not play the flute.)

Sagittarius, the centaur,
hoofs dust and cat hair
onto the spot of the basement
that was mine before college.
(The cat has moved out as well tonight,
                             symbolizing patience.
The basement is my brother's dominion tonight,
                             symbolizing a rib-stuck arrow
                             that symbolizes abandoned orbitals.)

Orion, the hunter,
plans to fleece my golden cheap necklaces
untangles them with large thumbs
and garlands the remains along his belt.
(The necklaces are all shaped like typewriters tonight,
                             symbolizing egotism.
The necklaces were all broken by tonight but I kept them anyway,
                             symbolizing breaking what I love
                             and keeping it anyway.)

Gemini, the twins,
let the confused silverfish
I flicked out the window
crawl from arm to arm to arm to arm.
(The silverfish is not silver tonight,
                                  symbolizing comedy.
The window is painting springtime tonight,
                                  symbolizing all the things I should
                                  avoid jumping out of

or into
                                  this spring.)

LISTENING TO SOUL
Matt Spencer

I was listening to old Soul songs when it occurred to me that there's a difference between "that's something that I'd like to do" and "that's something that I'd like to do, with you"; a howling void.
Of all of those "somethings," falling in love is the most coveted, the one we most want to possess, to consume down to sun-bleached bones devoid of marrow and cracking under the weight of gravity, collapsing into themselves.

Love is not a dog from Hell, it's a car-struck stray decaying in a desert like a deeply cliché landscape painting.

There's meaning in that, in the way some things just live and at the end just die, no grand narrative, no autobiography. It's nothing to cry about, things run their course, diminishing returns. At the end of the day this is air, it's left to us to interpret. Love is like that, at least in our art-cinema dreams.

"Dream a Little Dream of Me" is just desperate enough to be a great love song; one lover asking another to please let them sink into their subconscious, please think of me when I'm not around, please tell me that your mind always returns to the thought of our love.

There's a lot of fabrication, destruction, refabrication of words that grasp and claw at meaning but never manage to get a hold; all of it churning, consonants and vowels huddled against the stagnant cold of meanings, real and imaginary, fixed and fluid, all of it failing to pour out what it was Sam Cooke asked/commanded/begged when he sang the combination of words that to us means "bring it to me, bring that sweet lovin', bring it on home to me," or when Otis Redding confessed "I've had nothing to live for, looks like nothin's gonna come my way," but I've felt the hot breath and bitten shoulders, the sublime necessity of skin rubbing skin and the voice calling from far in the past to love and love wholly, love with an ache that seizes the vocal cords and contorts the body like being consumed by a holy spirit.

I want to see it like something within grasp, something in three dimensions; not like the way we see stars, virtually.

BREAKFAST AT ZOTO'S
Vijay Singh

Into the beauty
Of the moment,
Mind was drawn;

Light stilled;
Time stopped;
Past and future
Were no more;
Millennia traversed,
Or maybe just an instant

Finally, spell broke
As the wind arrived;
Light shimmered; creation
Began to quiver; and then,
In rising sound, the swaying
Of trees, branches and leaves

DIALOGUE
Bronson O'Quinn

This page was written
with 3,542 lines
of complete gibberish.
But you only see
     9
because we're both
too deep
in conversation
to care.

DREAM FRAGMENTS
~ *An erasure from Jane Hirshfield's "Sky: An Assay"*
Karen George

the room opens   to sky

a snake twisted   on a model's shoulders
    tender as hope

through the window   a harbor radiates

a mountain proposes to the moon

ENJAMBALAYA
Deborah Adams Cooper

Begin
with
the holy
trinity

add fish
stock

spices

meat

rice, cook
'til
thick

Enjoy
with
wine and
write.

FREE WILL
Amy Camuglia

There is no law against hatred
And none against forgiveness

GRANDE DAME
Beatrice Underwood-Sweet

I have lived in cities.

In Los Angeles with its
brash youth, gaudy lights,
and serpentine freeways.
Luring you in with promises of fame
only to spit you out forever changed.

In Oklahoma City, its near
perfect grid marred
only by the collision of
air from north and south,
its red dirt like earth's blood
welling up, scars laid open across
its sprawling spaces.

Oh, but the city of my heart
is Lexington,
grande dame of the south.
Her streets laid out like spokes,
history scribed in every curve.
She captivates with Southern charm
until you've drowned in her embrace.

HOW TASTES CHANGE, OR DO THEY?
Mary Allen

In my days of playing dress-ups and admiring Nancy Drew,
I decided the grown-up me would be a Girl Detective.
I'd wear black sheathe dresses and sandals with 4" heels like
those donated to my cache of finery by Mother's friend Odee.
I'd drive a Cadillac convertible, black, of course,
but never exceed a self-imposed 40 mph speed. I'd tail subjects
into dim-lit bars and sip martinis while chanteuses sang
throaty ballads of longing for loves gone wrong.

Now Kinsey Milhone supplants the dream of Nancy Drew.
Dresses give way to jeans, heels to Nike gels. The convertible
morphs to a venerable Honda sedan, dusty brown, impelled
by my heavy foot. I sport black underwear and am held
in thrall by the artistry of Diana Krall. And martinis?
Tanqueray Rangpur, over ice, with a twist.

I MET GOD—SHE'S BLACK
Bianca Spriggs

Up until now, I have always believed
I would know the face of God when I saw it.
I had no idea that when we met,
she would look just like me.

IN FAIR VERONA
Jonel Sallee

Fair Verona is unseasonably hot today,
Swelters under a loft of high pressure
That sends salty rivulets down reddened cheeks
And shortens breaths straining to escape hot lungs.

    Yet at *la casa di Giulietta,* the queue still lengthens,
Winding its way through the courtyard, past the balcony,
That famed meeting place of lovers' eyes.
The faces of the pilgrims have the look of believers,
As each, in quest of true love,
Touches Giulietta's bronze breast,
Now shiny and garish as the sun

    While I, longing for nothing more than a cool breeze,
Sit in the shade of a sycamore tree as the line lengthens,
Fan the air a bit with my city map, and whisper,
Caro Dio, fellow travelers! Do you not know
How this story ends?

LITTLE NO PEEP
Catherine Perkins

she
dangles from the rafters
of life
on strands of hard work
spun as strong
as spider's silk
feeling not so hale
hearty or tough
as in days
of long past
she
longs for change
love and contentment
she craves
painless days
she starts to sway
back and forth
on her
strands of back
breaking work
in hopes that someone
will notice
she bangs and beats
the heavy wooden beams
shaking her world
in hopes that someone
will hear
her distress
she doesn't utter a word
she doesn't run away
she hopes that someone

will know her plight
and cut
her umbilical cord
of manual labor
she hopes
that without a sound
someone
will set her free
so that she may find
a new identity

LOATHSOME CREATURES
Serena Devi

when they can't find the moon,
they bay like stray dogs at the crooning of police sirens
that lap at the milky night sky.
they are called loathsome creatures,
cast away and left to howl
until the roofs of their mouths collapse.

METAPOEM II
Sayid Bnefsi

she was not just
a gender-specific pronoun,

but also the subject of
poetic predication.

rising tension, she was
sometimes a metaphor,

sometimes a description,
we were in love like

like I was
in love when she was in love.

but dénouement,
and an ambiguous conclusion

expressing equanimity
or just equanimity.

NAKED BODIES
Rayny Palmer

I've only seen
you naked
twice.

You've seen me
many more.

I don't think
we have a
good relationship.

ON AN OTHERWISE CLEAR CLOUD-LIT NIGHT
Douglas Self

when the moon
dissipated
a great white shark

and

split a horseshoe
into parentheses
without so much

as a single touch

PALMOLIVE: ANNA AND JEAN-LUC
(Found and Fictionalized)
Chloe Forsting

She refuses the nude scene first thing.

He wonders if she can even sense
the heat of shame
growing on the back
of his thin, pale neck.

A little while later she is in front of him again,
seated (like him) on a café terrace
perfectly innocently.

The question comes to pass:

she once
played with soap bubbles
in front of a camera

as they frothed around her
like so much adoration

so why not undress
again?

And she says

Are you mad?

(Perhaps he is.)

I was wearing a bathing suit in those ads—the soapsuds went up to my neck.

(More shame—they did.)

It was in your mind that I was undressed.

(How could he be so dumb?)

PASTORAL
Gaby Bedetti

Driving through Bluegrass Station on Briarcliff Road
En route to Windy Corner Restaurant
We slow down

In the distance we see a figure chasing a puppy off the road
Through the trees we see a second figure seated
On the side of the road

Inspired by the horse farm fences
We wave to the person in the wheelchair
A legless man wearing a baseball cap

Did we see
What we saw?
We ride in silence

RED BIRD, BROWN BIRD
Joan Burke

already morphing into pressure—the day,
slipping away, late again.
outside this window, it's only June.

mourning doves graze, content, and then
red cardinal and little
girl cardinal are passing string? worm? via
tiny beaks, one, two, three bird-kisses!

all urgent tasks-to-be
dissolve
I am frozen in bird-land

inside the house
someone says
birds don't kiss
we are out of milk

SHUT UP
Marta Dorton

shut up

like a talker
who does not quit
jibber jabber jibber
the mockingbird
squalks
twert twert twert

perhaps by making
this connection
bark bark bark
the incessant situation
will sound better
chip chip chip chip
or worse

SOCCER IS LIFE
Duke Gatsos

A faded soccer ball
sits on Tates Creek at New Circle like
a lost child. Its black and white hexagon-pentagon pattern
swirls into gray gloam. Moms in minivans parade by,
passengers strapped carefully into backseats,
prisoners of suburban
parenting.

They hustle to practice
where coaches yell for speed and precision,
clamoring a championship. Day and night, they are smashed
into a wall over and over and over, juggled: drop—tap—lift,
plummet—bump—rise, fall—kick—ascend
until little Andrew wins
a scholarship.

Flat in the median
it soaks up sun memories
of when it was hugged two-armed to chest,
as toddlers rolled in the grass chasing it down a hillside.

SOMETHING OF WILD HOLINESS III
Kate Fadick

she dreams of a night spent
at sea

when the ship is hers
on watch

and wind makes of her hair
a pall to catch

dying stars she tastes burning
on her tongue

incense in a thurible awaiting
the evening

sacrifice of flesh become
word

STORM INTERLUDE
Roger Conner

Rain drops hang from
the screen gamely
seen through window
panes hanging on
soon to perish

A bird flies high
circling soaring
in victory
soaring circling
below dark sky

Circling clouds
rain drops and birds
do not depart
distant thunder
means birds and clouds
and rain drops too
have more to do

soaring
soaring circling
below dark sky
Circling clouds

rain drops and birds
do not depart
distant thunder
means birds and clouds

SUNDAY PAPER
K. Nicole Wilson

I am scaring the dog with my writer's block,
ripping pages of wrong-writing
into pieces as ragged as Colorado crags,
disturbing my little cow chaser's couch nap.

She starts, and then I do too,
apologizing first, with a good head scratch,
and then inking a salt-and-pepper spotted dog
in a land where everything is black and white

if I can find a way to say it plain,
and tell honest stories about love.

THE CAPTAIN DOES NOT UNDERSTAND THEIR SPEECH
jeremy dae paden

He has studied how verbs work on objects,
how agents act: God first formed man then woman,
then she took the fruit and ate, how God confused
their speech and sent them out into the world
as punishment but not before he cursed
the ground. How man is homo laborans,
how life is a pilgrimage, a search for God.

His mouth cannot make the taps, flaps and trills,
so closed and tight his tongue, the *wa,* small and soft
as wonder, is replaced by the constricting
velar *gua.* There is no order to this language,
he writes. What should go before, goes after.
One word can mean a thousand things, and the dead,
and the gods, who can tell one from the other?

What is this land where the solstice does not order
seasons, land where women tend *conucos*
that grow long, fat tubers? Where bread and drink
are made from poisoned roots, not from golden
seeds buried and born again? Where strange fruit
ripens year round on trees without labor
and reptiles are husbanded for food?

What is this *cacique* dance, *areíto?*
Why do all their songs sound like wind on water,
like the call of a lover at the sight
of his beloved leaving their bed at dawn,
like a meandering conversation
between the living and the dead, between gods
and those the gods protect, like waves on sand?

THE CHILD OF A GOD NAMED GOD
Tyler Worthington

Blood flows thicker than water
as does wine
A God named God
once turned Egypt's water into blood
some say A God named God still does that
from time to time
just to prove a point
all it takes is one fool
to never see the signs

after many battles fought
after A God named God drove the battle cries
of the ancient Israelite
a child of A God named God
killed a giant, who was a child of God too

the child left standing became a symbol for his peers
for children must be led by a child
long was his reign
every day the child fought
till nothing but an aged man
holding hands with an aging woman
were left to ponder what organized mess
they would leave behind

They had many children
but none for a long time
remained

it wasn't until another child came
that elders remembered
the giant killer's name
given to a star

funny how a child begat a child
in another time and place
this time no giant slayer came
only
A far seeing healer
or some might say a catalyst
so that nothing could ever be the same
the only child among children
who ever knew A God named God
just wanted to heal
the forgotten and displaced

this child ventured to Galilee
and found the town well
and turned the water into wine
when asked why
he said "hell …" and shrugged with an innocent grin
"I thought it couldn't hurt to have something safer to drink … and besides
it just might make you think"

it's no wonder
after so many children fell
for the ancient hate mongering spell
spat by High Priests of A God named God
and jeered at him
mocked him
tortured him
killed him
then locked his body away
the town of Galilee never again slept well

it was better in those days
to not speak of all children's rights
or a child's insights
although the organized mess we children have made
has changed after all this time
since when was the life of children peaceful?
since when has it been easy?

THE PAINTED FOREST
Robert S. King

Our stage of Everyman
has no music or balcony scene,
no Rapunzel's rope of hair,
no moral, no Moses
with stage direction tablets,
no swords to clang.
The set is cardboard, a watercolor
woodland scene where trees
huddle together in the rain,
a tombstone leans
from shallow roots,
the cricket crowd is quiet,
and owls don't care to ask.

The line feeder's script,
smeared from tears, dried long ago.
The audience snores but stays.
Wind quietly dies with the fan.
Sound effects have no effect.
One-hand claps fall on deaf ears.

In a three-act play, practice
never makes perfect.
The plot always leads
to the same conclusion
clad in worn-out costume.
No one calls for encore
in fear of the same ending.
Stage right and left the actors walk
off without bowing, forgetting
their parts in the death scene,
knowing that a good tragedy

must end in silence, perhaps
with a songbird dead in the dirt
of an empty forest
and the audience gone home
to their familiar graves.

THE SECTION
Erin Chandler

There is a home nestled beneath a thousand pines
In the home is an area
The area is divided into two sections

I fancy my section a Parisian flat
Velvet pillows, Oriental rugs and Sterling silver
My stepsister doesn't fancy her section
She boxed herself in with a bookshelf and two brown dressers

My section has two dogs and a cat
Her section has earplugs

"I have to stay close to my higher power or I will lose it!"
Bottles of Lithium, Clozapine and Seroquel on her bedside table
Make me believe her

"I will slip into such a deep depression, you don't even know"
I do, but perhaps not to the extent that makes her throw her hands up
Pray to God and Joel Osteen

It's a comfortable sort of prison
Thrown into intimate space with another fractured adult
Silent husbands and children in our wake, we wait

With only one thing in common
We forgot to grow up
Somehow missed the turn off

A murmur of Christian music comes from her section
She reads *The Shack* for the second time in forty-eight hours
Yards away but worlds apart
I read *Confessions of an English Opium Eater*

We're both trying to quit smoking

THINKING OF LARGE NUMBERS
bront davis

Thinking of large numbers
Those that exist among zero
And one and
Two and three

I've always been troubled by
Notions such as these
Each number like a cardboard box
Overflowing with the water of tiny infinities

The game box had masking tape
At the corners holding it together
How much age can a body hold
Before it falls apart?

In those days we wore the Scrabble tiles blank
With our contemplative counting fingers
Then made whatever words we wanted
And stopped keeping score

Conversing while the rain
Ran down our windows
On what we imagined
Were endless afternoons

UNCLEAR COASTS
Joseph Allen Nichols

> "Don't grieve. Anything you lose
> comes round in another form."
>
> —Rumi

I don't believe in this
idea of reincarnation, of
birth in new or varied forms
once we've uncoiled
the spool of a lifetime—

    yet here we are
    again, exchanging
    familiar faces

tracking traces, reading
the once have beens, the
breadcrumbs of forgotten
fairy tales, in media release
& foot prints, pressed in
the myriad greys
of obits—

    and I am alight,
    the moonbow, tip-toeing
    the edges of someone
    else's fall.

And you are rising, diaphanous
from noctilucent waters
below highway one,
  and the cliffs,
    with a kiss

      from the Pacific
          sun.

★ ★ ★

meadow dawn smith

i'm just sitting here.
think they've forgotten.

in recent days,
my lines are more pronounced.

wonder if they noticed.

dark spots blotch,
my picture of perfection.

clouds upon my sunnier days.

do they know i'm sweeter now?

  —banana thoughts

WHAT LIES BENEATH
Pamela Gibbs Hirschler

A bound book.

A blank page.

A pencil.

A glass of wine.

Time.

Record what simmers beneath
rotting tree limbs, old tires,
unmatched shoes, a broken doll,
wreckage of all sorts, and
don't forget the bodies
the current stripping away flesh
until only polished bones remain.

How else to encounter
what lies beneath
than to explore the depths?

WHEN THE IDEA OF LOVE HOUNDS AROUND
Savannah Sipple

remember the throe, the throb
down in your spine—it clutched
you like an orange rind—remember

it and how your stomach lurched
when you first learned love could
end. Don't let it wrack its way

to you. Don't let it hatch. Forget
heat that sears through fingers,
a fast moving ore, don't want

more. Forget the way it pulses. Don't
let it sap you. Don't throw
the dog a bone—it bites.

Tuck that heart-singe close
to you. Keep it fresh at your side
like a fish at rest in a creel.

WILD CANARY
Chaiya Miller

Why strive to capture
what's not meant to stay—

stay present, don't look away
to reach for a lens or pick up a pen

if you are able, don't even blink—
let the image keep, let the vision linger.

per-chik-o-ree, per-chik-o-ree, per-chik-o-ree

YOU IN THE MORNING
Laurel Dixon

You skin the plum with the slice of your teeth
delicate nails grazing the purple flesh
your head bent over your day's first labor
hail to the woman who may yet tease splinters
from the pads of her fingers
who wields the tools
who carries the hammer

Teach me how to find a table on the curb
and call it beautiful
Teach me how to straighten its broken legs
paint the round oval of its face
like rouging a woman's cheeks

like you gripping my chin
painting my eyelids with sharp black wings

Teach me how not to love you in the morning
How to forget your cold-plum silence
Your silhouette hunched before the bay window
Your hands braced
against the golden glass

MAN HOLDING BREATH IN OREGON TUNNEL CAUSES CRASH
Leigh Anne Hornfeldt

The tunnel carries the highway
772 feet through mountains.
That's 10 seconds of held breath.
10 seconds of wish. What did he want?
A new job, more money? For his golden retriever's bone cancer
to stay in remission? I like to think it was love.
That maybe he saw the face of a shy red head,
her thin lips as they mouthed the words I do
before he blacked out and everything went dark
around the edges, a photograph on fire. His wrists lax
at the wheel as his Camry drifts sleepily to the left.
What does a 19-year-old know except invincibility?
How could we expect him not to believe
his wish would come true? On the other side of the road
an elderly couple in a Ford Explorer. Certainty
bears down on them like a pinprick of light.
No hope of escape.

KENTUCKY
S.R. Gollihue

Sitting on the porch swing
Listening to whippoorwills call out
from treetops I can't see.
Honeysuckle air and lightning bug stars
But you are so much more.
You are real and you are poetry
You are home.
I am rooted to you.
I have mountain blood.

OFF THE TABLE
Linda Caldwell

After making several 360 degree
turns in less than five minutes,
Mayfrey uprights herself
over the cross-hairs.

The technician reaches
to help her stand.

She says, "You are so tiny and cute."

Not something Mayfrey wants to know
at almost seventy.

A QUESTION
Zlatna Kostova

> to K.

I have a friend
who knows
how God punishes.

Tell me, my darling,
will the man
who threw away
a stray cat's newly-born
be punished?

Memory

ANCESTRAL QUESTION
George Ella Lyon

Papa Dave's older brother Claude
married and moved to California
from the mountains of Tennessee.

Word of Claude never scaled
the Rockies or rippled Kansas wheat
until his unnamed wife poisoned him
with a piece of peach pie. No one knew
where they lived, no one knew why he died.
How did they know it was peach?

IN THEIR ELEMENT
Pat Owen

Turtles in their element,
heads emerging to meet raindrops.
Steady rain on the lake—
Even the golfers have given up.
White pennant flaps in the distance.
Song lyrics surface
"When will my soul get it right?"

Three years to recover—
to even consider looking
toward connection.
Threat of grief stronger
so far, than need.

Raindrops patter on the lake,
on the tile roof.
The primordial longing
begins its glacial birth.

USE FOR XANAX #212
Keith Stewart

It's that time of night when the butterflies soar
from the heart of my stomach to the gut
of my mind,

anxious Monarchs of worry unlocking
the chains where my demons are contained
freeing them to flood my brain

with their "what-ifs" and flutter my heart
by their "you forgots" until my lungs
can barely keep pace.

These butterflies know all the moves
to this game, they know they'll lose
their strength and control

over my system. These terrorizing Monarchs
have very short life spans, but my peach
pill helps finish them off even faster.

I settle back into bed, confident
my internal locks are now medically sealed
and feel the last butterfly slowly close its wings.

WOMEN, BREAD AND BLOOD
Milena Valkanova

Mom, there are times
when your hand in mine
feels like throbbing
of a thousand lives together.
We are the unsundered
chain of blood
meandering
within the riverbeds
where our great grandmothers
threw their daughters like bread
on the water.
Now is a time
to let your mother walk
on the Dead Sea of your tears
toward the dawn of forgiveness,
so that you can grow,
so that our women's blood
is purified
and continues its way
to my future daughters
and she, and you, and we
come back again
like bread on the water.

★ ★ ★

Barry George

It's midsummer's eve—
let's all put our pj's on
and watch the fireflies!

DOVES, GONE
Ann Neuser Lederer

Where are the doves of yesteryear? Their soft coos
lulled us to sleep at night, woke us each morning.
Their sudden silence slowly dawned.
Their murmurs replaced by raucous caws
of crows establishing in rafters of the empty,
crumbling house across the street.
Did the crows scare off the doves?
Did the doves grow weary of their calls?
Once, the doves routinely wandered
in the dusty driveway, usually at dusk.
We had gotten used to their apparent fugue states,
grew fond of their aberrant behaviors.
Now, we wonder what their absences might signal.
Canaries, bees, or insignificant lives?

FAIRYTALE
Elizabeth Kilcoyne

tell me a story about heaven;
the bruised peaches and blackberry wine
our bodies bathed in sudden rainwater
lightning crackling safe on the horizon.

tell me about the heat of summer
blistered and backed up against the chain link fence
the peeling red honeycomb scabs on your elbows
your raised scars fresh and foxglove pink

help me to remember the sweetness
forget the sour plum skin stuck between your teeth
the way our bodies stayed bodies for such a long time
our innocence had to be identified by the dental records.

leave out the hell that came later,
the soured milk solid and reeking in the broken bottle,
your dog dragging his withered flank into your basement
where we'd passed out drunk just to sleep at your feet.

tell me about the morning right before,
when we woke up like siblings in shared sheets
the fluttering in my throat that might not be terror
might not be love, the surety that this was good.

tell me what you remember of the words i gave you.
knowing that the good things only lasted through stories
carving us into your skin like a stick-and-poke tattoo.
letting us last beyond the ruin of it. giving us a chance.

LETTING GO OF DICHOTOMIES: THE NATURAL WAY TO END WAR

Marvis Lisso Hartman

In my first life,
I was Medusa's
hairdresser.
You would think
I'd be ready
for anything,
but it takes effort
in this life
to coil the polar opposites at each end of a continuum
so that the head
swallows
its own
tail.
It is only
when half-asleep,
resting
between worlds,
that I recall
how to think
from the middle out
like a
snake.

FOOD DEPOSITORY OF CHICAGO
Rudy Thomas

When we entered the building,
the lady behind the desk at the main entrance
told us to go to the first room on the left &
wait for her.

We were a group of 13: 4 staff & 9 students serving
one week of community service, foregoing romance
in favor of feeding the needy &
giving of ourselves for the good of another.

Our host informed us we would be boxing carrots
that would be distributed to the needy throughout
Chicago's diverse neighborhoods.
She told us 30 persons normally box three tons.

Applying Henry Ford's assembly line to carrots,
we organized, prioritized, & set about
our task at hand. Other groups boxed other foods,
breakfast, for the most part. We set a goal, four tons

& no less. We worked. We learned. We made boxes.
We piled one pound & two pound bags on our lines.
We made adjustments. We sorted, counted, labeled
& when our shift ended, we had boxed 11 tons.

HARD
corey kirby

apartment empty
cept white shelf
bought from asian
student

bathroom mirror
still reflect
you n him
brushing teeth

wallpaper dark
where wedding photo
hung

by stove
your ghost arms
wrap his ghost waist

by sink
his ghost palms
grasp your ghost breasts

on kitchen counter
your ghost mistake
making love
with being love

you pick up final bag
pull door shut
hard

but do not lock it
it is anyone's
for taking

ANTIPODE
Jay McCoy

When I was nine, I wanted to be
Cherokee more than anything—
I wore my fringed navy suede vest
all the time, kept Billy ThunderKloud
& the Chieftones on my red molded
plastic compact phonograph, even
once talked my father into a stone
tomahawk on a visit to the Smokies.
I often thought about traveling
to the other side of Earth. Today,
I googled it & discovered I would
have ended up deep in the Indian
Ocean had I bored my way through.

LIFE CYCLES AND HABITATS (A SEQUENCE)
Matthew Haughton

1. Relocation

Be it long winter
or short fire,
houses
and hornets
will repopulate.

2. Territory

I do not know for whose life
this all belongs.
If I've made a home here,
it was to watch the vetches
strain into existence.

3. Architectural

The house binds itself
to the landscape,
hornets spin in the eaves.

4. Waiting

If the house seems
too quiet,
it is because
the mowing
outside ceased.

I've grown close
to what
happens now,

to this span
of silence until rain.

5. Silk Caps

If only all things could begin
with the eagerness
exhibited by hornets,
chewing the lids off their cells.

FORGET-ME-NOTS
Nettie Farris

I can't say
that I was ever fond
of that photograph.
It isn't Billy.
Not the Billy I knew.
Some people called him
the Robin
Hood of New Mexico.
But when I think
of Billy, I see the blue
of his eyes, the color
of the wide western sky,
(freedom) the color
of cornflower;
and I hear
the sweetness
of his voice
singing to me in Spanish.
I feel his arms
encircling
me while dancing
and the curve
of a six-shooter
on his right hip.
You can't resist
a boy who loves his mother.
I thought he
would hang,
but Billy
was a great
escape artist,

and the vistas
of New Mexico are vast.
I had no premonition
he would die
in my own house.
Not Billy.
I had no premonition
he would die
at all. And now,
sometimes, as I lift
the tea cup to my lips
during the lull
in a conversation,
I can hear the hooves
of his horse
clapping the earth
(like the roll
of the timpani,
echoing),
and I'm not sure
whether they are moving toward
or away from me.

PORTRAIT OF MY MOTHER AS A DRIED SUNFLOWER HEAD
Pauletta Hansel

The round shape of you
no longer round,
bent in on yourself
as if you are trying to find your way
back to the place you began.
You smell of dust
and still that scent
of only you.
I cannot see what you were
in what I have before me,
though in dreams you still stand
tallest in the field.
Every day a little
more of you
is gone. You are
beautiful.
You are so beautiful.
At the center,
a constellation of seeds
never planted.

FOUND IN HER BAGGAGE
Sherry Chandler

a limestone rock
a stem of mock orange blossoms
a Baptist hymnal
a raptor feather
a weathervane in the shape of a cock
a dressmaker's tape
a souvenir salt shaker
a faulty windfall peach
the false-leather fringe of a Dale-Evans skirt
the flirt of a fan
a hillside white with Queen Anne's lace
the filigreed hands from the face of a clock
a dead ex-husband's blame
the stick-figure gallows from a Hangman game
fat leeches from a shallow creek
a barn owl's midnight screech

FUNERAL WISHES OF A MODEST MAN
Ryan D. Mosley

When my humble pass halts
like a summer struck by year's first frost—
When unending silence befalls the resting chair
that creases childlike smiles with yarns
spun to warm our common air—
When my pockets are empty of Kentucky's bitter strands—
When they no more make a home for the impatient hands
that move the politics of our cresting lands—
When the Precious Hymn cues a procession to be led
by grandsons carrying the final bed—
When my time amongst men comes to a stop,
lay me up on a mountaintop
under a blanket sewn of fragile, brown nettles
that drift like snow to the feet of pines,
whose permanent shadow is cast unbothered
by the toiling mines.
Where hills are fed to skies,
and Silent Death settles well
into the lungs of men
who cough the tune of His Early Bell.
When I am returned to Gaia's bowels—
silence your wails and mute your howls.
Make your faces like Troublesome in drought.
And celebrate a life you'll soon be without.

JOHN REID JUMPS AN IRON HORSE
David Cole

Train track train track unused
but for freight and one man lone.
Hustle along for two centuries
still running but not the same,
folks forget what you're for.
Now just freight, one man lone.
When it came roaring through
Danville nights, I, up with no
sleep no sleep for train track
whistle out there, loud loud
from one man lone, one machine
calling out for some wise ass
kid to hop on and ride awhile.

I trailed along behind, hid
between twisted trees of winter
and dead plant on ground and I
hopped up and made that train
track track carry on for freight
and two men. Lone.

LOST LOVE
Patrick Maloney

when i go
outside to get
high, alone

i watch the flowers
i picked for you
die. They bow

to under the ground
even while they're
lifted in the sky.

ONE DAY I TOOK MY POEMS INTO AN EMPTY ROOM
Tina Parker

I lined them up in rows
Many different rows
I lined them up and closed the door
They never said a word

POEM 10
Elizabeth Beck

    for Shuntella

do you remember when
we would play kickball
in the cul-de-sac? we
cried do-over! car!
hold the ball, stop
the game. started over
until someone's mom
called out names
for dinner. twilight.
lightning bugs. ghost
in the graveyard. statues.
disputes decided in rocks,
paper, scissors. judicious
calls for red rover, red rover.
studiously stepping over
cracks that broke our mothers'
backs. we sipped from garden
hoses and lived

REMEMBER WHEN
yahieisha adams

Remember when we was kids
Remember when we used to stare at one another
Remember when we used to see each other at the park
Remember when we would try to speak to each other but we was so shy
Remember when we got to sat beside each other
Remember when we didn't see each other anymore as kids
Do you remember

Remember when I grew up
Remember when I used to be a tom boy
Remember when I stopped being shy
Remember when I had so many friends
Remember when I knew myself
Remember when I met all the wrong guys
Remember when I became damaged
Remember when I got pregnant
Remember when I got kicked out of the house
Remember when I was homeless
Remember when I had to stay with friends
Remember when I had my son
Remember when I was alone
Remember when I was blessed with a place
Remember when I was always a giver
Remember when I went back to Jesus

Remember when you wrote me out the blue
Remember when you acknowledged us being shy when we were kids
Remember when you and I exchanged numbers
Remember when you and I talked all night long
Remember when you used to try to hang up and couldn't
Remember when you and I hung out for the first time
Remember when you first kissed me

Remember when you looked at me with so much love
Remember when you knew me and I knew you
Remember when you loved me
Remember when you left me
Remember when you turned your back on me
Remember when you started talking to my friend
Remember when you act like I was nothing to you
Remember when you tried to play me
Remember when you tried to sabotage my new relationship with a lie
Remember when you had me
Remember when you…..
I could go on and on but
Remember when I went to God and he wiped my tears and he healed me and gave me peace.
I forgive you I do
I'll always remember when

REMEMBERED
Dennis Preston

The tombstone reads,
"1929 – 1997."
The date of his birth
seems important;
so does the date
he died. The only thing
that represents his life
is a hyphen.
The years of school,
work, raising a family,
good and bad decisions,
epitomized
by a small dash
carved into granite.
I hope someone
remembers more.

SEVEN MONTHS INTO FOREVER
Naomi Clewett

Enervated
by store after garish store
of ill-fitting pants

blindsided
as I reach the car
I weep

remembering all those clothes
you bought without me,
how perfectly they fit.

All the way home
I cry, grateful
for this grief,

its sting, for the sudden
upwelling of pain
proclaiming your loss,

redeemed
for the moment
from the terrible ease

with which the world
without you
became normal.

All the way home
I cried, two hours,
the last time

we saw you
alive. Slipping
away

gradually
before our eyes;
suddenly

it seemed
you had crossed
a line.

SHE AIN'T EVEN FROM LEXINGTON
Liz Prather

we don't hear fresh life
coming up in the making
a little foot stomps at the Kimball House
and a darkish eagle egg,
corrected in limestone
sheds its gray leather tack
monkeys swung from wire to wire
for a clean water bucket
sunk from McConnell's Springs
back to who we once were
broken, 1985, at the Bluegrass Airport
remembering the broad way
where shufflettes posed
with drag queens
under the t-barred windows
tilled early, harvested late
working root to bear rubies,
the simplest shade
in the valley
delight of a wild life
an unspeakable vision
looking back from C.V. Whitney's limo
as we sleeked by.

STROKE
Nora Burton

I

At the end my mother lay

on her back paralyzed, unable
to see or hear.

She is comfortable
a smiling nurse tells
us while removing
her ventilator and disconnecting the IV tube.

Death watch, we wait

as her chest rises and falls
until we hear in the space
between exhale and inhale
a sigh like the one a mother
makes when the umbilical cord
is cut and her child floats free.

II

Two days after she died
we gathered at her house
and cried while my father
unlocked her jewelry chest
motherless my siblings and I
sat at the dining room table
and received pieces of her jewelry
the ones she said she wanted
each of us to have. By the end
of the day my father had given
everything that had once been hers away.

THE EDGE
M J Eaton

Of a leaf
sharp ridged moist
cutting through the air
piercing the sweet scent
of clover and fern.

Of a cloud
creating a golden line
when seen between
the sun and sky
grey to white and
between full of rain.

Of a bird
the line changing
as the movement of wings
progress and light.

Of a wind
shredded by flight
scents a part
and different from the moment
of the first feel.

Of a memory
painful at first
soothing when time
has gone
forever there even as
years make the speaking
of it silent.

THE MOURNING WOMEN
Kristy Horine

Consider and call down the Mourning Women,
the ones who professionally wail.

Gather 'round :
the trees you planted,
the garden you tended,
the rocks you stacked,
the sticks you gathered
that built
the fire
you were supposed
to burn
on your anniversary.

Wail out the injustice
of never ever after.
Wail out the pain
of other togethers.
Wail out the anger
that droops into sadness
and caves in the chest—
rounded shoulders and bowed head and clench-closed eyes and fisted
hands and memory, memory, memory.

That baby loves you,
he said one time
when the sleep still clung to my skin, my hair, my eyes;
(the child we made rested on the hill
of the bed where we made her;
the hill between my side and his)
She doesn't know what love means,
I said, and knew what I really meant.

She opened her hand,
he said.
Love is an open hand?
I said.

Yes, love is an open hand.

And the Mourning Women came,
dressed in bird clothes,
and sang through the window:
"Charity, charity;
charity, charity."

And then, I closed my eyes and waded into the wails.

THE WITCH'S HOUSE
Kristine Nowak

was across the fence at the far side
of the kickball field—through the trees,
you could see the roof slanting down
into the porch, the tangles of weeds among
the stairs, the black cat staring hungrily
into the schoolyard—a few times, I even saw
the witch herself: alone, hunched in her black clothes
under a nest of gray hair, tending her garden
of strange and gnarled plants.
The older boys threw stones, the girls
just whispered, huddled by the fence
to look. Now that I am older, I understand
why a woman might stray from precisely
what is expected of her, might choose to grow
wild and mossy plants with hidden blooms
instead of pink petunias and fuchsia,
why she might choose to let her hair and skin
crackle with age, keep a cat too sweet
to be unlucky. I do not think she was anything
other than a woman without a language
small enough to explain herself to children, to explain
how a garden, watered and tended, might bloom
in uncountable different ways.

★ ★ ★

Carmen Norris

chipped fingernail polish
riot grrrl mix tapes
zines and thrift store dresses
all the good things have stayed the same

WRONG STATION, OLD NOTEBOOK
Bernie Deville

Angels fall
like grace
from a ghost
selling sanctuary—
scar tissue to treasure
like the cracked pages
of a found book
wedged between
the headboard
and the wall.

NOT AN EASY MAN TO LOVE
Bobby Steve Baker

I was guilty knew damn well I was guilty
of having "got above my raisin'" bad when family sucks you in
when I arrived I heard clumps of mourners muffle a concurrence

the red-eye from LA to Toronto was late to take off
doing surgery all day I nearly missed visitation a compulsory
in the morbid exercise to get the mean old bastard in the ground

I chose the two lane lakeside route to my hometown
hauling ass in a huge black Lincoln rented in deference
to nothing but deference itself given I was not bedside when …

which put me up shit-crick and this overblown casket of a car
was no paddle for getting back down or where ever
you try to get to when you're up the crick I wouldn't know

I remember roiling black angry clouds coming in
slow off the lake to rain seething sheets over it all
the lying in the cucumber sandwiches the funeral the burial

he would enjoy all of us got soaked to our fucking
underwear to see him off in all propriety slogging
through the mud of a fresh grave site to throw a rose

now my sister tells me it was a brilliant blue late august day
not a cloud in the sky kind of cliché day I actually
don't remember anything except lifting and holding

his dead hand and rolling his Masonic Lodge ring
in my fingers sobbing uncontrollably until my cousins
wrapped around me and sat me down a fatherless child

ON TIME DILATION
Eduardo Ballestero

Think, for a moment,
of the two brothers
in the twin paradox.

How long they hugged
before the one separated
from the pull of this world.

How the twin in space
touched the screen each time
he spoke to his brother,

and tears dulled his sight
when he traced each new
laugh line and wrinkle

that revealed how much
more his brother had aged.

How the twin on Earth,
who'd married, had children,
and lived so fully for both

him and his brother,
felt his breath catch in his throat
whenever the two spoke—

heartened by the belief
that time was only something
that could touch those of us

who were still bound
by the weight of the Earth.

ABOUT THE POETS

Mary Allen lives in Lexington. She's a member of the writing group Bluegrass Wordsmiths, and she comes to poetry through study with poets at the Carnegie Center.

yahieisha adams is the mother of one, a handsome son. She believes in God and graduated in 2010. She loves to write and talk. She also loves to read poetry.

tina andry is the author of *ransom notes*. she has two children, likes haircuts (sometimes) anime, & old-fashioneds.

Jenni B. Baker is the editor-in-chief of *The Found Poetry Review*. Her work has been published in more than a dozen literary journals. To learn more, visit *jennibbaker.com*.

Bobby Steve Baker has lived in Lexington for 30 years, with a summer home in his native Canada. He enjoys being part of this vibrant Arts Community.

Eduardo Ballestero was born in San Carlos, Costa Rica and grew up in Kentucky. He has a B.A. in English from the University of Kentucky and lives and works in Lexington. He is at work on a collection of persona poems.

Jennifer Barricklow is a poet and editor living and writing in the Bluegrass.

Leslie Bartley: Limp-wristed queer with a rusty terrace!

Allie Marini Batts is managing editor of *Zoetic Press* & the *NonBinary Review*.

Elizabeth Beck is a writer, teacher and artist.

Gaby Bedetti is a long time professor in the English Department at Eastern Kentucky University.

Sayid Bnefsi studies philosophy at Berea College, speaks French, and writes poetry despite the availability of Netflix.

Maggie Brewer is originally from Worthington, Ohio. She moved to Kentucky to attend Transylvania. She teaches high school history and lives in Frankfort.

Mattie Bruton is nineteen and enjoys ghost stories and spending time with arthropods.

Jennifer Burchett: writer of prose, maker of soup, not a poet, living in the beautiful Bluegrass.

Joan Burke was born and raised in Kentucky, went to UK, lived in New York and Lake Tahoe, California, where she met her husband. They moved back to Lexington years ago with kids in tow. She loves Lexington and California.

Elizabeth Burton is a student of English at Lexington's own Transylvania University. When she is not writing poetry she is watching magical girl anime.

Nora Burton holds an MFA in Creative Writing from Murray State University, is the author of two memoirs, numerous essays and selected poems.

Linda Caldwell: writer of poetry for many years.

Amy Camuglia was born Amy DeMoulin, but in the mid-west, so her french name was always pronounced "dee-mo-lin." Unfortunate! Her hubby and she drive a hand-painted car.

Sherry Chandler has lived long enough to accumulate considerable baggage. Her latest book, *The Woodcarver's Wife* (Wind Publications), celebrates 40 years of letting things accumulate in the same place with the same man.

Erin Chandler: primarily a writer of creative nonfiction, she is also a playwright and actress and has produced theatre and independent film. Her first book, *June Bug Versus Hurricane* will be coming out soon.

Chuck Clenney hails from Covington and now resides in lovely Lexington, Kentucky. By day, a Japanese translator, other times, visual artist, poet, radio DJ, and word nerd. He does a radio show on WRFL 88.1FM every Tuesday from 10-Midnight.

Naomi Clewett is a Lexington native who has an MFA in creative writing from the University of Alabama. Her poems have appeared or are forthcoming in *Puerto del Sol, Georgetown Review, Dialogist, DIAGRAM, Southern Poetry Review* and elsewhere.

David Cole: recently voted the worst-dressed sentient being in the universe for the seventh time running.

Roger Conner was born in Central Kentucky, studied Humanities as part of Honors class at Elizabethtown Community College

Deborah Adams Cooper is the author of *Letcher County: Images of America* (Arcadia Publishing, 2011). She has forever been amazed by words and the power and possibility they hold. In her youth she could always be found with a dictionary by her side. She writes poetry in Cynthiana, Kentucky.

Taylor Emily Copeland is a poet from Eastern Pennsylvania. Her chapbook *Caffeine kisses and long sleeves* is available through Maverick Duck Press.

Sean L Corbin is a member of the University of Kentucky MFA program in Creative Writing. His work has been places.

bront davis: In progress ...

University of Kentucky graduate **Andrew Depew** writes and lives in Lexington, Kentucky.

Serena Devi: SCAPA Literary Arts student, lover of poetry, music, dogs, and all things colorful.

Julian DeVille is an honors student at Eastern Kentucky University double majoring in math and electrical engineering, but still longs for the liberal arts.

Bernie Deville is a Montessori Middle School teacher and MFA student at Eastern Kentucky University.

Laurel Dixon has had her poetry published in *Tobacco Magazine* and *Miss'ing Magazine*. She spends most of her time reading, gardening, and drinking too much coffee.

Marta Dorton is a writer and visual artist living in Lexington. She writes memoir and arts articles, creates acrylic paintings at her LAL studio and printmaking pieces at the BPC.

M J Eaton's books include *For Poets, Grab Me a Bus,* and *Feeling-My-Way*. She has taught at Drake, UALR, Carolina University, UMKC. She was the first woman Poet in the Schools in Kentucky. She has received 14 grants from NEA and is working on her next colleciton.

HB Elam is a Kentuckian, Transylvania graduate, Lexington ex-pat, bluegrass lover, verbose grammarian, coffee drinker.

Kate Fadick's poetry is influenced, in part, by her experience as a community organizer in Eastern Kentucky (Jackson and Owsley Counties) and urban neighborhoods in greater Cincinnati.

Nettie Farris lives in Floyds Knobs, Indiana and is the author of *Communion* (Accents Publishing, 2013). In 2011 she received the Kudzu Poetry Prize. Her work has been nominated for a Pushcart Prize. *Fat Crayons* (largely composed during Lexington Poetry Month 2013) is forthcoming from Finishing Line Press.

Matt Finley is from London, Kentucky. He has published flash fiction for *Winged Nation* magazine at the College of William and Mary and for *Readwave.com*, for which he is an editor. He also has a J.D. from the College of William and Mary Law School and lives in Virginia.

Chloe Forsting is a student writer. She's working on it. She can be a real jerk about music but otherwise she guesses she's okay.

MC Spam Bot has recently started a blog, the information you offer on this website has helped him tremendously. Thank you for all of your time & work!

Morghan Fuller is an English Teaching major from Lexington, entering her junior year at Eastern Kentucky University. This is her second year participating in Lexington Poetry Month.

Duke Gatsos lives in Lexington, Kentucky, finishing a Ph.D. in higher education. BAs in Religion and English. Works at UK as student support in Educational Leadership. Writing more consistently for the last 6 years.

Karen George, author of *Into the Heartland, Inner Passage, Swim Your Way Back,* and *The Seed of Me,* has work published in *Memoir, Louisville Review, Permafrost, Still,* and *Wind*. She reviews poetry at *Poetry Matters,* and is fiction editor of the journal *Waypoints (www.waypointsmag.com)*. Her website is *karenlgeorge.snack.ws*.

Barry George's haiku and tanka have appeared widely in anthologies and journals, including Japanese, Chinese, German, Russian, and French translations. He is the author of *Wrecking Ball and Other Urban Haiku* (Accents Publishing), nominated for a Pushcart Prize, and *The One That Flies Back My Way* (Kattywompus Press).

S.R. Gollihue is a native Kentuckian who loves being surrounded by the mountains and trees of her hometown. She lives with her husband, their two cats, and their dog.

Jaria Gordon: A mother, student, and writer from Lexington, Kentucky.

Pauletta Hansel is a writer, teacher and author of *Tangle,* out in 2015 from Wind Publications, *The Lives We Live in Houses* (Wind Publications, 2011) and *What I Did There* (Dos Madres Press, 2011). She edits *Pine Mountain Sand & Gravel,* the literary publication of Southern Appalachian Writers Cooperative.

Matthew Haughton's two poetry books are *Stand in the Stillness of Woods* and *Bee-coursing Box.*

Pamela Gibbs Hirschler is a Kentucky native who lives in Frankfort. She works in information security and writes poetry and fiction.

Cheyenne Neckmonster writes things. They are sometimes true.

Kristy Horine writes; therefore she is a writer. Sometimes she writes her stories. Sometimes the stories of others. Sometimes those stories even look like poems.

Leigh Anne Hornfeldt is a Pushcart Prize & Best of the Net nominee and the author of 2 poetry chapbooks.

Carole Johnston drives around the Bluegrass and Eastern United States with her camera and notebook in the front seat of her car, always ready to capture that "aha" moment. Her collection of poems, *Journeys: Getting Lost* will be published very soon by Finishing Line Press. She is grateful because many of the poems in this volume were written for Lexington Poetry Month 2013.

Elizabeth Kilcoyne is a poet and playwright from Central Kentucky. She is a graduate of the University of Kentucky with a B.A. in Theatre. She is an alumni of Governor's School for the Arts and The Twenty: A Young Writers' Advance. Elizabeth currently lives in Lexington, Kentucky.

Robert S. King: Editor of *Kentucky Review* and author of eight poetry books, most recently *Developing a Photograph of God* (Glass Lyre Press, 2014). His poems have appeared in hundreds of magazines.

Corey Kirby is a full-time social worker, part-time writer. She draws inspiration from the South, traveling, and the everyday bravery of ordinary people.

Michelle Knickerbocker is a quirky poet living in Frankfort. She grew up in Florida and still enjoys fresh citrus and sunshine. She think spiders are neat but doesn't want them near her. Her favorite color is green.

Zlatna Kostova: Anchored 2 talkshows on RFE. Translates poetry, fiction, TV programs, movies and plays. Author of poetry book *Sparrow in a Shell*. Since 2007 has been Director at BTA. Bulgarian.

Jude Lally fulfills his creative, expressive and therapeutic needs by writing about family, travel, romance, nature and, of course, his disability, a rare neuromuscular condition called Friedrich's ataxia. Although he moved around a lot growing up, he never lived more than 75 miles away from where he currently resides, in Lexington, Kentucky.

Jim Lally wakes in the mornings to the sound of rooster crow. He falls asleep in the evenings to the melancholy coo of mourning dove.

Ann Neuser Lederer was born in Ohio and has lived and worked in Lexington for 20 years. See *ann-neuser-lederer.blogspot.com* for details about her poems & nonfiction.

George Ella Lyon, the author of four poetry collections (most recently *Many-Storied House*), she makes her living as a freelance writer and teacher based in Lexington.

Patrick Maloney is just a tiny human like you who likes to write.

Erin Mathews: nineteen, a Kentucky-raised and Ohio-bound English major caught somewhere between a wild-haired youth and crotchety old person.

Jay McCoy: bookseller by day, poet by night.

Christopher McCurry is an Editor at Accents Publishing, an advocate for poets at the Field Office, and a high school English teacher.

Chaiya Miller has called Lexington home for over 35 years.

Samantha Jean Moore: This Modern Nomad May Forever Wander, but if she ever makes her way back Home, she'll be headed to Lexington.

Ryan D. Mosley is from Emmalena, Kentucky and lived in Lexington from 2011 – 2015. He writes poetry about his home in Knott County. He will be attending Cornell University Law School in August 2015.

J W Mullins is an author, photographer, poet, apologist, husband, and daddy. He loves his wife's passion, the laughter of his children, poetry, and Jesus Christ unabashedly.

Sue Neufarth Howard: Poet, visual artist; member—Greater Cincinnati Writers League (GCWL) and Colerain Artists. Published in *Her Limestone*

Bones: Lexington (Kentucky) Poetry Month 2013; High Coupe and *Cattails* online journals; *AEQAI* online magazine; the *Journal of Kentucky Studies;* the *Mid-America Poetry Review;* and *The Incliner—Cincinnati Art Museum.*

Joseph Allen Nichols lives in Lexington, Kentucky. He writes poetry, long and short fiction, as well as nonfiction. He meditates to the sound of two wild boys and his dog, Lorelei. He is currently finishing his thesis and MFA degree with The Bluegrass Writers Studio at Eastern Kentucky University.

Carmen Norris is a tooth collector, adventurer, cat lady, fashion lover and secret writer. She enjoys hanging out with her cats, reading outdated self-help books, and stargazing.

Kristine Nowak grew up in Washington and moved to Kentucky in 2008. She currently works in a library and lives in Lexington with her husband, dog, and two cats. She writes poetry.

Bronson O' Quinn loves lots of things, but mostly books.

Andres Ortiz Lemos: Quito, Ecuador.

Pat Owen holds a JD and MA in English from University of Louisville and has done graduate work in the MFA program of Spalding University and has been published in *The Louisville Review.* Her book of poems *Crossing the Sky Bridge* has been accepted for publication by Larkspur Press.

Jeremy Dae Paden: poet, professor, pater familias, poacher of eggs, pesto pounder, and procrastinator extraordinaire.

Rayny Palmer: Creative Writing major at SCAPA; sixteen; *Lord of the Rings* fanatic; cool kid in the making.

Tina Parker lives in Berea, Kentucky, with her husband and two young daughters. Her chapbook *Another Offering* is available from Finishing Line Press. Her full-length poetry collection *Mother May I* will be published by Sibling Rivalry Press in 2016. For more about Tina, visit *www.tina-parker.com.*

Jen Parks, as a full-time working mother of three small children, uses writing, running, and copious amounts of chocolate to give balance to her daily life. She is an MFA student at Eastern Kentucky University.

Catherine Perkins is a 58-year-old woman who started writing as a tormented teen. She continues to attempt expression through writing and poetry.

Liz Prather grew up in northern Fayette County on a tobacco farm and attended University of Kentucky. A writer and teacher, she now lives in eastern Kentucky.

Dennis J. Preston is a native Kentuckian living in Owensboro. Retired from teaching, he pastors a small, rural church. He received his doctorate from Louisville Presbyterian Theological Seminary, and enjoys reading, writing, traveling, and spending time with his daughter, son-in-law, and grandson. He has published poems in *The Lumberyard*, and *Trajectory*.

Melva Sue Priddy lives in Winchester, Kentucky. She earned an MFA in Writing from Spalding University. Writing is one of her main loves.

Robin LaMer Rahija is the editor of Rabbit Catastrophe Press.

Katie Riley co-leads Poezia, a poetry workshop that welcomes all poets (Common Grounds Coffee House, Thursdays at 7 pm). Her poems have appeared in *Still: The Journal*.

Jonel Sallee: in ninth grade, an aptitude test said that she should be a writer. Instead, she spent nearly a half century trying to teach others how to write. Oh, well.

Douglas Self: human being.

Vijay Singh is a dreamer-poet in his leisure hours and a research scientist in professional work. He works at University of Kentucky as a Professor of Electrical and Computer Engineering.

Savannah Sipple is a poet from Eastern Kentucky. Her work has recently been published in *Still: The Journal*, and *Deep South Magazine*.

meadow smith, born and reared in the bluegrass, branched out for a stint here and there, called to come back home—first time submitting, feeling about as comfortable as microwaved foil.

Matt Spencer will soon begin a Ph.D. program in English at Middle Tennessee State University. He will be moving out of the great state of Kentucky for the first time in his life to do so.

Kate Spencer moved from the Midwest plains to the heart of the Bluegrass in 2005, beginning a period of repeated transitions. These inspired an appreciation of art and ignited her own creative flame. As a psychologist, she incorporates both into the work.

Bianca Spriggs is an Affrilachian Poet and Cave Canem Fellow. An award winning poet, Bianca is the author of *Kaffir Lily* and *How Swallowtails Become Dragons*.

Jay St. Orts: Husband, Father, Son, Brother, Uncle, Friend, Musician, Homebrewer, Cook, Editor, Writer. Not necessarily in that order.

Keith Stewart = Poet. Writer. Blogger. Good Eater. Bad Singer.

Travis Stidham is the founder and host of the monthly reading series, Treehouse Poets Series, in Hazard, Kentucky.

After living in Lexington for 20 years, **Karah Stokes** lives and gardens in Frankfort, in a house festooned with cats. She is learning to play clawhammer banjo.

Katerina Stoykova-Klemer is a Bulgarian from Kentucky.

Victoria Sullivan is an Appalachian writer of poetry and fiction from Vanceburg, Kentucky. A recent graduate of Transylvania University, she plans to pursue her MA in English.

Eric Scott Sutherland is the creator and host of the Holler Poets Series. His latest collection of poems, *pendulum*, was recently released by Accents Publishing.

Rudy Thomas has published poetry, short stories, and a novel online, in journals, as well as 25 books. His work has often been anthologized. He is also the founder of Old Seventy Creek Press.

Alexis Tipton: 14 years old. I like to ride horses.

A displaced Kentuckian living in Oklahoma, **Beatrice Underwood-Sweet** has been published in *Her Limestone Bones* and *The Sun Magazine*. She hopes to never lose her sense of wonder upon publication.

Milena Valkanova is a Jungian analyst in training and a psychological astrologer who would give a sociable vent to inner images, voices, screams and laughs through verses.

J. Wise: Teacher, aka the great American hustler: pedagogical Butch Cassidy, literary Sundance Kid; walking thesaurus/dictionary; critical reader; bad dancer; dreamer of impossible dreams.

Maggie Wells is a native who loves this state, the earth, her family, and all things innovative and creative. Most of the time she's a teacher, but she's always a mother and a writer.

Shuntella Whitfield was born and raised in Lexington, Kentucky. She is the mother of two beautiful children, daughter Kira (14), son Devin (12). She is lover of poetry, dancing and fitness.

K. Nicole Wilson is a Maysville (aka Limestone), Kentucky native, and after living out West for seven years, she's become an immoveable Appalacian mountain. A permanent part of the scenery.

Tyler Worthington is a senior at the University of Kentucky majoring in Anthropology. Lexington is my hometown, and I love to spend my time immersing myself in art, music and literature.

ABOUT THE EDITORS

Christopher McCurry lives in Lexington, Kentucky with his daughter and his wife, where he teaches high school English and is an editor at Accents Publishing. His poems have appeared in *Limestone, The Los Angeles Review, Rabbit Catastrophe* and others. His short story, "Those Who Trespass Against Us," won the *Still: The Journal's* 2013 fiction contest. He is working on a master's degree in English literature, thanks to a fellowship from the CE&S Foundation, at the Bread Loaf School of English.

Hap Houlihan is the general manager of Lexington Community Radio. He has been a reader at the Holler Poets Series since 2010 and was a featured Holler Poet in June, 2012. He lives in Lexington, Kentucky with his wife Lori and his sons Murphy and Simon.

Robin LaMer Rahija is the editor of Rabbit Catastrophe Press.

ACKNOWLEDGMENT

We would like to express our heartfelt gratitude to the following organizations and businesses who made this project possible:

www.ingramcontent.com/pod-product-compliance
Lightning Source LLC
Chambersburg PA
CBHW021151080526
44588CB00008B/293